Explorers on Safari

Sally Hewitt

illustrated by Serena Feneziani

Thameside Press

Tell the time with the explorers

At dawn the explorers are fast asleep. Cook bangs his frying pan to wake them up for breakfast. Will today be the day they spot the rare giant gorilla?

A clock on each page shows you the time. What time do the explorers reach the ravine? When do they swim in the lake? What time is bedtime?

Look for the gorilla. He's too smart for the explorers—is he too smart for you?

At the end of the day the explorers set up camp and get ready for bed.

At dawn the sun rises on a new day.

Will the explorers see the giant gorilla today?

Cook bangs his frying pan. "Good morning. Time to get up!"

What time do the explorers get up?

Mr. Magill is trying to get dressed too quickly.

Scout is still in his pajamas.
What should he put on first? What next?

"Breakfast is ready!" shouts Cook.

Who has dressed and washed faster?
Who is slower?

Skipper and Susie are early for breakfast.

8:00

eight
o'clock

Who is on time for breakfast?
Who will be late?

Skipper calls a meeting. "We must find that gorilla!"

What time is the meeting?

Skipper points to today's plan. **9:00**
"Any questions?" she asks.

nine o'clock

What day is it today?
What did the explorers do yesterday?

The explorers pack up their tents for the trek.

Who will take longest to pack?
Who will take less time?

Poor Cook!
Look at his enormous load!

Who is ready to go?

At last, everyone is ready.

Who is leading the expedition?
Who is last in line?

Susie is on her first safari.

Which equipment looks brand new?
Which looks old?

At noon the explorers reach the ravine.

How will they cross the ravine?
What time does the clock show at noon?

14

Suddenly the bridge breaks in two!

Who took the shortcut?

Now it's afternoon.
The explorers stop for lunch.

Who is the last to arrive?

"Still no sign of that gorilla," grumbles Skipper.

Who is already eating lunch?

After lunch, the explorers take an afternoon nap.

How long do you think they will sleep?

Time to move on.

2:00
two
o'clock

Who would like to sleep a little longer?

19

Look out, Susie!

Tell the story of what happens to Susie.

Oops! Ouch! Splash!

What will Susie do now?

The others jump in the lake too!

What time is it now?

"We have to reach the camp before sunset," cries Skipper.

Skipper is ready to go.
Who will be ready last?

"Keep looking for the gorilla," shouts Mr. Magill.

Follow the path from the lake to the new campsite with your finger.

"Last one to reach camp does the dishes!" yells Skipper.

Who has gotten stuck? Who is racing along?

They arrive tired and hungry.

What will the explorers need to do before bedtime?

Susie unpacks her knapsack.

Find everything she needs for the night.

Susie looks at her photos.
"There's the gorilla!" she laughs.

5:00

12:00

2:00

8:00

Point to the day's photographs in order.
What happened first?

The explorers go to bed early after their trek.

What time do the explorers go to bed?
When is your bedtime?

The explorers fall asleep quickly.

eight
o'clock

How do you know that it's nighttime?

Notes for parents and teachers

Explorers on Safari will help your child to:

- Learn and use words about time.
- Begin to read "o'clock" time.
- Become familiar with digital clock faces.

- Sequence familiar events.
- Learn to use words about speed.
- Begin to know the days of the week in order.

The sun rises over the camp at dawn. Learn about breakfast time, morning, noon, lunchtime, afternoon, sunset, and bedtime as the explorers spend a day trekking. Look for two kinds of clock face at the top of the pages and learn to read "o'clock" time. The explorers keep missing the gorilla—can you spot him?

Start the day with the explorers as Cook wakes them up for breakfast.

- Help them put on their clothes in order.
- Find out who is early and who is late for breakfast.
- Look at Skipper's plan and learn about yesterday, today, and tomorrow.

- Sort out Susie and Mr. Magill's old and new equipment.
- Tell the story of how Susie fell into the lake.
- Find out who is fast and who is slow as they hurry to the new campsite.

Mr. Magill

When Susie looks at photographs of the day's trek, she has a surprise. Are the explorers alone as they settle down to sleep?

Cook

Try these activities and games to help you learn about time.

• Spot clocks everywhere you go. Talk about when it is important to know what time it is.

• Make a clock face and attach hands with a paper fastener. Turn the hands to show different times on the clock.

• Keep a diary. Write down important events and interesting things that happen to you each day.

• Use a digital stopwatch or a clock with a second hand to time a race with a friend. See who can do the most skips, put on the most clothes, and so on—in 10 seconds, 30 seconds, or one minute.

Susie

Scout

Skipper

31

Distributed in the United States by
Smart Apple Media
1980 Lookout Drive
North Mankato, MN 56003

Text by Sally Hewitt
Illustrations by Serena Feneziani

Series editor: Mary-Jane Wilkins
Editor: Russell McLean
Designer: Jamie Asher
Educational consultant: Andrew King

ISBN: 1-930643-56-X
Library of Congress Control Number: 2001088838

Printed in China

9 8 7 6 5 4 3 2 1